PRINCEWILL LAGANG

Driving Change: Rob Walton's Leadership Journey at Walmart

First published by PRINCEWILL LAGANG 2023

Copyright © 2023 by Princewill Lagang

All rights reserved. No part of this publication may be reproduced, stored or transmitted in any form or by any means, electronic, mechanical, photocopying, recording, scanning, or otherwise without written permission from the publisher. It is illegal to copy this book, post it to a website, or distribute it by any other means without permission.

Princewill Lagang asserts the moral right to be identified as the author of this work.

First edition

This book was professionally typeset on Reedsy.
Find out more at reedsy.com

Contents

1	Introduction	1
2	The Early Days	3
3	Navigating the Winds of Change	5
4	Global Ambitions and Corporate Responsibility	7
5	Innovations and Challenges in the Digital Age	9
6	Reinventing Retail: Rob Walton's Legacy and the Future of...	12
7	Continuity and Evolution: Walmart's Next Chapter	14
8	Reflections on Leadership and Legacy	17
9	The Ever-Evolving Retail Landscape	20
10	The Next Frontier: Challenges and Opportunities in 21st...	22
11	A Lasting Legacy: Rob Walton's Impact on Retail and...	25
12	Charting a Course for the Future	28
13	The Intersection of Leadership, Innovation, and Social...	30
14	Summary	33

1

Introduction

"**D**riving Change: Rob Walton's Leadership Journey at Walmart" invites readers on a captivating exploration of one of the world's retail giants, Walmart, and the transformative leadership journey of Rob Walton. This narrative spans decades, tracing the evolution of Walmart from its humble beginnings to its current status as a global retail powerhouse.

In the opening chapter, readers are introduced to Rob Walton, who assumed leadership at Walmart in a pivotal era of the early 1970s. The narrative unfolds against the backdrop of a rapidly changing retail landscape, characterized by shifting consumer behaviors, technological advancements, and globalization.

As the inheritor of his father Sam Walton's legacy, Rob faced the challenge of not only sustaining Walmart's success but also driving meaningful change. The introduction sets the stage for a detailed exploration of Rob Walton's leadership style, strategic decisions, and the dynamic interplay between Walmart's growth and the ever-evolving demands of the retail industry.

The reader is guided through the foundational years of Walmart, witnessing the hands-on approach and innovative thinking that marked Rob's early leadership. The narrative captures the essence of Walmart's commitment to providing value to customers and the unique challenges faced by the company in adapting to an increasingly complex and competitive market.

This introduction serves as a gateway to a multifaceted journey, offering a glimpse into the intricate tapestry of Walmart's history and the visionary leadership that has shaped its trajectory. As readers embark on this exploration, they are encouraged to delve into the subsequent chapters that unfold the narrative of Rob Walton's leadership journey and its profound impact on Walmart's evolution.

2

The Early Days

Title: "Driving Change: Rob Walton's Leadership Journey at Walmart"

As the sun dipped below the horizon on the small town of Bentonville, Arkansas, a legacy was born that would forever reshape the retail landscape. In the heart of this quaint town, a young visionary named Rob Walton began his leadership journey at the helm of what would become one of the world's retail giants – Walmart.

The year was 1971, and Walmart, founded by Rob's father, Sam Walton, was already a growing force in the retail industry. Rob, armed with a fresh perspective and a keen sense of innovation, stepped into the role of leadership within the company. Little did anyone know that this transition would mark the beginning of a transformative era for Walmart and the retail sector as a whole.

This chapter delves into the early days of Rob Walton's tenure, exploring the foundation upon which he would build his legacy. We follow his journey from the corridors of the family-owned business to the dynamic world of retail, where challenges and opportunities awaited.

In the opening pages, we witness Rob's keen understanding of the changing landscape of retail. The 1970s marked a pivotal moment in the industry, with shifting consumer behaviors and technological advancements setting the stage for a retail revolution. Rob, with a forward-thinking mindset, recognized the need for Walmart to evolve and adapt to these changes.

The narrative unfolds against the backdrop of Walmart's humble beginnings, where the company's focus on providing value to customers resonated with the American middle class. Rob Walton, inheriting his father's commitment to customer satisfaction, began shaping a vision that extended beyond the confines of the small Arkansas town. The first chapter navigates the reader through the corridors of the early Walmart stores, showcasing Rob's hands-on approach and commitment to fostering a culture of excellence.

As we delve into the chapter, we witness the challenges faced by Rob Walton in steering Walmart through an era marked by economic uncertainties and changing consumer preferences. The narrative captures the essence of his leadership style, characterized by a unique blend of strategic foresight, adaptability, and a deep-rooted commitment to the values instilled by his father.

The chapter concludes with a glimpse into the strategic decisions that laid the groundwork for Walmart's expansion into a retail powerhouse. From embracing technological innovations to redefining supply chain management, Rob Walton's leadership journey in these formative years sets the stage for the transformative changes that would unfold in the subsequent chapters.

"Driving Change: Rob Walton's Leadership Journey at Walmart" begins with a captivating exploration of the early days, providing readers with a nuanced understanding of the man behind the vision and the pivotal moments that would shape the future of retail under his guidance.

3

Navigating the Winds of Change

Title: "Driving Change: Rob Walton's Leadership Journey at Walmart"

As the 1980s dawned, a wave of change swept through the retail industry, and Rob Walton found himself at the helm of Walmart, steering the company through uncharted waters. Chapter 2, "Navigating the Winds of Change," unveils the challenges and triumphs that defined this pivotal decade in Walmart's history.

The chapter opens with a snapshot of the economic landscape of the 1980s, characterized by global economic shifts, technological advancements, and a rapidly evolving consumer culture. Rob Walton, now firmly established as a leader, faced the daunting task of not only sustaining Walmart's success but also propelling it to new heights.

The narrative delves into the expansion strategies employed by Rob during this era, exploring the decision-making processes that led to Walmart's growth beyond its regional roots. From opening new stores to embracing innovative marketing techniques, this chapter paints a vivid picture of Rob's strategic acumen and his ability to navigate the complexities of a changing marketplace.

One of the central themes of this chapter is the technological revolution that swept through the retail sector. Rob Walton, recognizing the potential of emerging technologies, spearheaded initiatives to integrate cutting-edge systems into Walmart's operations. The implementation of barcode scanning, computerized inventory management, and early experiments with point-of-sale systems marked Walmart's commitment to staying ahead of the curve.

Amidst these technological advancements, the chapter also explores the human side of Walmart's growth. Rob Walton's leadership style comes to life as he fosters a sense of community and teamwork within the organization. The reader is taken behind the scenes, witnessing the collaborative efforts that fueled Walmart's success and contributed to its reputation as an employer of choice.

As the narrative unfolds, the reader witnesses the challenges faced by Rob Walton in balancing the pursuit of growth with the preservation of Walmart's core values. The chapter delves into the delicate dance between expansion and maintaining the "Everyday Low Prices" philosophy, a cornerstone of the company's identity.

The closing pages of Chapter 2 leave the reader on the edge of anticipation, as Rob Walton's leadership sets the stage for the transformative changes that would define the following decades. The narrative teases at the challenges and opportunities that awaited Walmart on the global stage, offering a glimpse into the dynamic leadership that would shape the company's destiny.

Chapter 2 encapsulates a decade marked by innovation, growth, and the indomitable spirit of a leader committed to steering Walmart through the winds of change. As Rob Walton's journey continues, so does the evolution of Walmart into a global retail powerhouse.

4

Global Ambitions and Corporate Responsibility

Title: "Driving Change: Rob Walton's Leadership Journey at Walmart"

As the calendar turned to the 1990s, Rob Walton's leadership at Walmart entered a new phase, marked by global ambitions and a heightened focus on corporate responsibility. Chapter 3, "Global Ambitions and Corporate Responsibility," unfolds against the backdrop of a rapidly globalizing world and explores how Rob Walton steered Walmart towards becoming a key player on the international stage.

The chapter opens with Walmart's bold foray into international markets, a strategic move guided by Rob's vision for expanding the company's footprint beyond the borders of the United States. The narrative takes the reader on a journey through the challenges and triumphs of Walmart's global expansion, from navigating diverse cultural landscapes to adapting business strategies to suit the unique needs of international markets.

Rob Walton's leadership during this period is characterized by a commitment to responsible business practices. The chapter explores Walmart's initiatives to enhance sustainability, reduce environmental impact, and address social issues. Rob's dedication to corporate responsibility is highlighted through the implementation of initiatives such as community outreach programs, ethical sourcing, and environmentally conscious business practices.

Against the backdrop of Walmart's global expansion, the narrative zooms in on the complexities of managing a massive and diverse workforce. Rob Walton's leadership style comes into focus as he strives to maintain a sense of unity and shared purpose across the expanding Walmart family. The chapter delves into the challenges of leadership in a multinational corporation, exploring how Rob fostered a culture that valued diversity and inclusivity.

As the 1990s progressed, Walmart faced increasing scrutiny on various fronts, from labor practices to environmental concerns. The narrative doesn't shy away from addressing the controversies and challenges that accompanied Walmart's rise to global prominence. Rob Walton's response to these challenges, his engagement with stakeholders, and the implementation of initiatives to address concerns are explored, providing a nuanced view of leadership under scrutiny.

The chapter concludes with a reflection on Walmart's evolving identity as a corporate citizen. Rob Walton's commitment to balancing the pursuit of profit with a sense of social responsibility sets the stage for the next chapter in Walmart's journey. The reader is left with a sense of anticipation, eager to discover how Rob's leadership will continue to shape Walmart's trajectory in the dynamic landscape of the 21st century.

Chapter 3 unravels the intricacies of Walmart's global expansion and the evolving role of corporate responsibility under Rob Walton's leadership. As the narrative unfolds, it becomes clear that Rob's vision extends beyond retail dominance, encompassing a commitment to ethical business practices and a positive impact on the global community.

5

Innovations and Challenges in the Digital Age

Title: "Driving Change: Rob Walton's Leadership Journey at Walmart"

As the new millennium dawned, the retail landscape faced unprecedented challenges and opportunities with the advent of the digital age. Chapter 4, "Innovations and Challenges in the Digital Age," chronicles Rob Walton's leadership journey at Walmart during a time of technological disruption and explores how the company navigated the complexities of e-commerce, digitalization, and changing consumer behaviors.

The chapter opens with the seismic shift brought about by the rise of the internet and e-commerce. Rob Walton, recognizing the transformative potential of digital technologies, steered Walmart into uncharted territory. The narrative unfolds against the backdrop of Walmart's endeavors to embrace e-commerce, from the launch of its online platform to strategic partnerships and acquisitions that aimed to position the company as a digital retail powerhouse.

Rob's visionary approach to technology and innovation comes to the forefront as the chapter delves into Walmart's efforts to integrate digital solutions into every facet of its operations. From supply chain optimization to personalized customer experiences, the reader witnesses the company's journey to redefine itself in the digital age. The narrative captures the challenges faced by Walmart in adapting to the fast-paced, ever-evolving landscape of online retail.

The human side of this technological revolution is explored as the chapter delves into the impact on Walmart's workforce. Rob Walton's commitment to talent development and fostering a culture of innovation is evident in the initiatives undertaken to upskill employees and embrace a digital mindset throughout the organization.

However, with innovation came challenges, and the chapter doesn't shy away from addressing the obstacles Walmart faced in the digital realm. From logistical challenges to increased competition from online retailers, Rob Walton's leadership is tested as Walmart strives to maintain its position as an industry leader.

A significant portion of the chapter is dedicated to Walmart's sustainability initiatives in the digital age. Rob Walton's commitment to corporate responsibility is reflected in the company's efforts to reduce its environmental footprint, explore sustainable sourcing practices, and contribute to social causes through technology-driven solutions.

As the chapter draws to a close, the reader is left on the precipice of anticipation, wondering how Rob Walton's leadership will continue to shape Walmart's trajectory in the face of ongoing technological advancements. Chapter 4 serves as a testament to the resilience and adaptability of Walmart under Rob's guidance, setting the stage for the next chapter in the ever-evolving story of Walmart's leadership journey.

Chapter 4 unfolds a narrative of innovation, challenges, and adaptation as

Walmart navigates the digital age under Rob Walton's leadership. The reader is invited to witness the intricate dance between tradition and transformation, as Walmart embraces digitalization while upholding its commitment to customer satisfaction and corporate responsibility.

6

Reinventing Retail: Rob Walton's Legacy and the Future of Walmart

Title: "Driving Change: Rob Walton's Leadership Journey at Walmart"

As the pages turn to the latter part of Rob Walton's leadership tenure at Walmart, Chapter 5, "Reinventing Retail: Rob Walton's Legacy and the Future of Walmart," delves into the culmination of decades of visionary leadership and explores the indelible mark left by Rob on the retail giant.

The chapter opens with a reflection on the transformative journey Walmart has undertaken under Rob Walton's guidance. It revisits key milestones, innovative strategies, and the resilience displayed by the company in the face of a rapidly changing retail landscape. The narrative unfolds against the backdrop of a world where the lines between physical and digital retail continue to blur, challenging established norms.

A central theme of this chapter is the evolving role of leadership in the 21st century corporation. The reader is given insight into Rob Walton's leadership philosophy, shaped by a commitment to values inherited from his father, a dedication to innovation, and a relentless pursuit of customer satisfaction. The narrative explores how Rob's leadership style adapted to meet the demands of an ever-evolving industry.

The chapter further delves into Walmart's ongoing efforts in corporate responsibility, sustainability, and community engagement. The reader witnesses how Rob Walton's legacy is not only about business success but also about creating a positive impact on the world. Initiatives related to environmental sustainability, philanthropy, and social responsibility underscore Walmart's commitment to being a responsible corporate citizen.

Amidst the successes, the narrative doesn't shy away from the challenges and controversies faced by Walmart during Rob Walton's leadership. From labor practices to criticisms of market dominance, the chapter provides a balanced perspective on the complexities inherent in steering a global retail giant.

As the narrative reaches its climax, the reader is presented with a glimpse into the future of Walmart. The chapter explores how the company, under the guidance of new leadership, is positioned to tackle emerging challenges, capitalize on new opportunities, and continue the legacy of innovation and responsibility established by Rob Walton.

In the closing pages, the reader is invited to reflect on the enduring impact of Rob Walton's leadership on Walmart's identity and the retail industry at large. The chapter serves as a bridge to the conclusion of the book, leaving the reader with a sense of closure on Rob Walton's leadership journey while igniting curiosity about the next chapter in Walmart's story.

Chapter 5 encapsulates the essence of Rob Walton's legacy, offering a panoramic view of the highs and lows, the innovations, and the enduring commitment to values that have defined Walmart's journey under his leadership. The stage is set for the final act, where the reader will witness the continuation of Walmart's narrative beyond the era of Rob Walton.

7

Continuity and Evolution: Walmart's Next Chapter

Title: "Driving Change: Rob Walton's Leadership Journey at Walmart"

As we turn the pages to the final chapter, "Continuity and Evolution: Walmart's Next Chapter," the narrative unfolds against the backdrop of a post-Rob Walton era. The reader is invited to witness the continuation of Walmart's journey, exploring how the company navigates the challenges and opportunities that lay ahead.

The chapter opens with a transition in leadership as a new figure takes the reins at Walmart. The narrative captures the spirit of continuity, acknowledging Rob Walton's lasting impact while setting the stage for a fresh perspective. The reader is introduced to the new leadership's vision and strategy, offering insights into how Walmart aims to evolve in response to the dynamic retail landscape.

A central theme of this chapter is the evolving nature of consumer expectations and retail dynamics. The narrative explores how Walmart, a retail behemoth shaped by the leadership of Rob Walton, adapts to emerging trends, technological advancements, and shifts in consumer behavior. From omnichannel strategies to the integration of advanced analytics, the reader witnesses Walmart's commitment to staying at the forefront of the retail industry.

The chapter delves into the global expansion efforts that follow Rob Walton's leadership, examining how Walmart continues to establish its presence in new markets while deepening its roots in existing ones. The narrative navigates through the challenges and triumphs faced by the company on the global stage, providing a comprehensive view of Walmart's role in an interconnected world.

Corporate responsibility and sustainability remain focal points in this chapter, underscoring Walmart's commitment to making a positive impact on society and the environment. The narrative explores new initiatives, partnerships, and innovations that further the company's dedication to responsible business practices.

As the chapter unfolds, the reader is presented with a retrospective view of Rob Walton's leadership, contextualizing his legacy within the ongoing narrative of Walmart. The reader witnesses the continuity of values established by Rob, now woven into the fabric of Walmart's corporate identity.

In the closing pages, the narrative invites reflection on the dynamic nature of leadership and the enduring legacy of a leader like Rob Walton. The reader is left with a sense of optimism about Walmart's future, having been guided through a comprehensive exploration of the company's journey, challenges, innovations, and commitment to driving positive change.

Chapter 6 serves as the epilogue to the leadership journey of Rob Walton at Walmart, bridging the past with the present and pointing toward the future. The book concludes with a sense of fulfillment, leaving the reader with a holistic understanding of Walmart's evolution under Rob Walton's stewardship and the ongoing narrative of this retail giant in the years to come.

8

Reflections on Leadership and Legacy

Title: "Driving Change: Rob Walton's Leadership Journey at Walmart"

In this final chapter, "Reflections on Leadership and Legacy," the narrative takes a step back to contemplate the broader implications of Rob Walton's leadership journey at Walmart. It is a chapter of introspection, analysis, and contemplation on the enduring impact of one man's vision on a global retail powerhouse.

The chapter begins with a retrospective examination of the leadership principles that defined Rob Walton's tenure at Walmart. It delves into the intricacies of his leadership style, drawing insights from key decisions, challenges overcome, and the core values that guided Walmart through decades of change. Interviews with colleagues, employees, and industry experts provide a multifaceted view of the man behind the leadership.

As the narrative unfolds, the focus shifts to the broader implications of Walmart's journey under Rob Walton. The reader is invited to consider the company's influence on the retail sector, its contributions to the global economy, and the ripple effects of its innovations on businesses and consumers worldwide.

The chapter explores the concept of leadership legacy, examining how Rob Walton's vision shaped not only Walmart but also the narrative of corporate leadership in the 20th and 21st centuries. Interviews with business scholars, analysts, and industry leaders provide diverse perspectives on the lasting impact of Rob Walton's approach to leadership.

The narrative delves into the role of leadership in driving change, not just within the confines of a company but on a societal level. Walmart's influence on employment practices, supply chain management, and community engagement becomes a focal point, prompting the reader to consider the broader implications of corporate leadership on the world stage.

As the chapter progresses, it navigates through the challenges faced by Walmart under Rob Walton's leadership, offering a nuanced perspective on the complexities inherent in steering a corporation of such magnitude. The reader gains insights into the lessons learned from setbacks, controversies, and the continuous process of adaptation in the face of evolving global dynamics.

The closing pages of the chapter serve as a platform for contemplating the future of leadership in the retail industry and beyond. The reader is prompted to reflect on the evolving nature of corporate responsibility, the role of technology, and the ethical considerations that will shape the next generation of leaders.

"Reflections on Leadership and Legacy" is a thoughtful conclusion to the book, inviting the reader to consider the broader implications of Walmart's journey under Rob Walton's leadership. It encourages introspection on the nature of corporate leadership, the impact of visionary leaders, and the ongoing narrative of change in the business world. As the book concludes, the reader is left with a sense of closure, having explored the rich tapestry of Walmart's evolution and the enduring legacy of one man's leadership journey.

9

The Ever-Evolving Retail Landscape

Title: "Driving Change: Rob Walton's Leadership Journey at Walmart"

This additional chapter, "The Ever-Evolving Retail Landscape," serves as an epilogue, providing a contemporary perspective on the retail industry and Walmart's role within it. As the book's narrative continues beyond the conclusion, this chapter explores the latest developments, challenges, and innovations in the retail sector.

The opening pages offer a snapshot of the current retail landscape, characterized by digital transformation, changing consumer behaviors, and unprecedented global challenges. The narrative explores how the industry has evolved since the conclusion of the previous chapters, setting the stage for an exploration of Walmart's continued adaptation to these dynamic changes.

The chapter delves into Walmart's strategies in response to the latest trends, including the integration of advanced technologies, data analytics, and artificial intelligence in its operations. The reader is given insight into how Walmart continues to innovate and stay competitive in the face of challenges posed by e-commerce, supply chain disruptions, and the demands of an increasingly interconnected world.

As the narrative unfolds, the focus shifts to the global perspective, examining Walmart's endeavors in international markets and the challenges and opportunities presented by diverse cultural, economic, and regulatory landscapes. The reader is invited to consider how Walmart's leadership, past and present, navigates the complexities of a world where borders are increasingly permeable, and consumer expectations transcend geographic boundaries.

The chapter also revisits Walmart's commitment to corporate responsibility and sustainability, providing an update on the company's initiatives to address environmental concerns, ethical sourcing, and social impact. Interviews with current leaders and stakeholders offer firsthand perspectives on Walmart's ongoing efforts to be a responsible corporate citizen.

Closing the chapter, the narrative prompts the reader to reflect on the continuous evolution of the retail industry and the role of leadership in steering companies through uncharted territories. The reader is left with a sense of anticipation, eager to witness how the retail landscape will further transform in the coming years and how Walmart, with its rich history and adaptive culture, will continue to drive change.

"Chapter 8: The Ever-Evolving Retail Landscape" serves as a dynamic conclusion to the book, extending the narrative beyond the initial chapters to provide a contemporary snapshot of Walmart's journey and the ongoing evolution of the retail industry. It encapsulates the essence of the book—change as a constant, and leadership as the driving force that shapes the trajectory of companies in an ever-shifting business landscape.

10

The Next Frontier: Challenges and Opportunities in 21st Century Retail

Title: "Driving Change: Rob Walton's Leadership Journey at Walmart"

This chapter, "The Next Frontier: Challenges and Opportunities in 21st Century Retail," propels the narrative forward, offering a forward-looking exploration of the retail landscape and the potential challenges and opportunities that lie ahead for Walmart and the industry as a whole.

The opening pages set the stage by examining the current state of the retail sector, identifying key trends, disruptions, and technological advancements that are shaping the way consumers shop. From the rise of artificial intelligence and augmented reality to the growing importance of sustainability and ethical practices, the reader is immersed in the dynamic forces reshaping the retail landscape.

The narrative then pivots to Walmart's response to these emerging challenges and opportunities. The chapter explores the company's strategies for staying at the forefront of technological innovation, adapting to shifting consumer preferences, and addressing the ever-growing importance of e-commerce in the retail ecosystem. Interviews with current leaders and industry experts provide insights into how Walmart is positioning itself for success in the coming years.

A significant portion of the chapter is dedicated to the role of leadership in navigating the complexities of the 21st-century retail environment. Drawing on lessons from Rob Walton's leadership journey, the narrative examines the qualities and strategies that effective leaders employ to guide their organizations through a rapidly changing business landscape.

The reader is invited to contemplate the implications of societal and environmental shifts on the retail industry. From the increasing demand for transparency and sustainability to the evolving expectations of the workforce, the chapter explores how companies like Walmart are adapting their practices to align with broader societal trends.

As the narrative progresses, the reader gains a sense of the interconnected nature of global business and the challenges presented by geopolitical, economic, and public health events. The chapter discusses how companies navigate uncertainties and build resilience to withstand unforeseen disruptions, drawing parallels with Walmart's historical responses to challenges.

Closing the chapter, the narrative leaves the reader with a sense of anticipation for the future. It prompts reflection on the evolving nature of retail and the leadership strategies needed to thrive in an environment of constant change. The reader is encouraged to consider how Walmart, with its legacy of innovation and adaptability, will continue to drive change in the years to come.

"Chapter 9: The Next Frontier" serves as a forward-looking exploration of the challenges and opportunities awaiting Walmart and the retail industry in the 21st century. It bridges the historical narrative with a future-focused perspective, inviting the reader to contemplate the continued evolution of retail and the role of leadership in shaping the industry's trajectory.

11

A Lasting Legacy: Rob Walton's Impact on Retail and Leadership

Title: "Driving Change: Rob Walton's Leadership Journey at Walmart"

In this final chapter, "A Lasting Legacy: Rob Walton's Impact on Retail and Leadership," the narrative concludes by examining the enduring influence of Rob Walton's leadership on Walmart, the retail industry, and the broader landscape of corporate leadership.

The chapter opens with a retrospective view of Rob Walton's contributions to Walmart and the transformative changes witnessed under his guidance. It explores how his vision and leadership style have left an indelible mark on the company's culture, values, and strategic direction. Interviews with colleagues, industry experts, and those who worked closely with Rob provide personal perspectives on the lasting impact of his leadership.

As the narrative unfolds, the focus expands to Walmart's place in the broader retail ecosystem. The reader is guided through an analysis of Walmart's influence on industry practices, its role in shaping consumer expectations, and the ways in which the company has set benchmarks for corporate responsibility and innovation. The chapter delves into the ripple effects of Walmart's strategies on competitors, suppliers, and the retail landscape at large.

The chapter also explores the evolution of leadership principles within Walmart and the retail sector, drawing a connection between Rob Walton's leadership style and the ongoing development of leaders within the company. It examines how his legacy has informed the next generation of executives, shaping the values and strategies that continue to drive Walmart forward.

A significant portion of the chapter is dedicated to Walmart's ongoing commitment to corporate responsibility and sustainability. The narrative details how the principles instilled by Rob Walton have become ingrained in the company's DNA, influencing its approach to ethical business practices, environmental stewardship, and community engagement.

As the chapter nears its conclusion, the narrative prompts the reader to reflect on the broader implications of Rob Walton's leadership journey. It considers the role of visionary leaders in steering corporations through periods of change, the lessons that can be gleaned from Walmart's story, and the continued relevance of the company in the evolving landscape of retail.

The closing pages offer a poignant reflection on the dynamic nature of leadership and the lasting legacy of Rob Walton. The reader is left with a sense of appreciation for the journey undertaken in this exploration of Walmart's evolution, recognizing the profound impact of one leader's vision on a global corporate giant.

Chapter 10 serves as the epilogue, providing a comprehensive and reflective conclusion to "Driving Change: Rob Walton's Leadership Journey at Walmart." It encapsulates the essence of the book, celebrating the transformative impact of Rob Walton's leadership on Walmart, the retail industry, and the broader narrative of corporate leadership.

12

Charting a Course for the Future

Title: "Driving Change: Rob Walton's Leadership Journey at Walmart"

In this additional chapter, "Charting a Course for the Future," the narrative extends beyond the historical exploration and legacy of Rob Walton's leadership, focusing on the strategic directions Walmart is taking as it navigates the evolving dynamics of the retail landscape.

The chapter begins by examining the contemporary challenges and opportunities facing Walmart. It explores how the company is adapting to the latest technological trends, consumer behaviors, and global economic shifts. Interviews with current leaders shed light on the strategies in place to maintain Walmart's competitive edge and relevance in an ever-changing market.

A central theme of this chapter is Walmart's commitment to innovation. The narrative delves into the company's initiatives in technology, e-commerce, and supply chain optimization. It explores how Walmart is leveraging data analytics, artificial intelligence, and other cutting-edge technologies to enhance the customer experience, streamline operations, and stay ahead of industry trends.

The reader is invited to explore Walmart's international footprint, examining the challenges and successes the company encounters in various global markets. The chapter provides insights into the ways Walmart tailors its strategies to meet the unique demands of different regions, embracing cultural diversity while maintaining a cohesive global identity.

Sustainability and corporate responsibility remain integral components of Walmart's identity, and the chapter offers a contemporary perspective on the company's efforts to address environmental concerns, support local communities, and promote ethical business practices. The reader gains insight into how these initiatives align with evolving societal expectations and contribute to Walmart's role as a responsible corporate citizen.

As the narrative unfolds, the chapter considers Walmart's role in the digital age, exploring the integration of online and offline retail strategies. The reader is immersed in discussions about the omnichannel approach, the importance of seamless customer experiences, and the ways in which Walmart is leveraging its vast physical footprint alongside its digital presence.

Closing the chapter, the narrative offers a glimpse into the future of Walmart and the retail industry. It prompts the reader to consider the ongoing evolution of consumer preferences, the potential impact of emerging technologies, and the strategic considerations that will shape the next chapters of Walmart's journey.

"Chapter 11: Charting a Course for the Future" serves as a contemporary addendum to the book, providing a snapshot of Walmart's current trajectory and its strategic responses to the challenges and opportunities of the 21st-century retail landscape. It extends the narrative beyond the historical exploration, offering the reader a dynamic perspective on Walmart's ongoing journey.

13

The Intersection of Leadership, Innovation, and Social Impact

Title: "Driving Change: Rob Walton's Leadership Journey at Walmart"

In this additional chapter, "The Intersection of Leadership, Innovation, and Social Impact," the narrative dives into the evolving role of leadership in the context of contemporary challenges and opportunities. The chapter explores how Walmart, under new leadership, continues to shape its identity in an era marked by the intersection of business, innovation, and social responsibility.

The opening pages set the stage by examining the broader landscape of leadership in the 21st century. The narrative delves into the qualities that define effective leadership in an era characterized by rapid technological advancements, global interconnectedness, and heightened social awareness. Drawing parallels with Rob Walton's leadership principles, the chapter explores how leadership styles have adapted to meet the demands of a fast-paced and dynamic business environment.

A central theme of this chapter is the symbiotic relationship between innovation and social impact. The narrative delves into how Walmart, as a global corporate entity, is leveraging innovation not only for business success but also to address societal challenges. From sustainable business practices to initiatives that promote diversity and inclusion, the chapter offers insights into how Walmart is aligning innovation with a broader commitment to social responsibility.

The chapter explores the concept of shared value, where businesses actively contribute to societal well-being while pursuing economic objectives. Through interviews with current leaders, the narrative provides examples of how Walmart is integrating social impact initiatives into its core business strategies, fostering a sense of purpose that goes beyond profit margins.

As the narrative unfolds, the focus shifts to the ever-expanding role of technology in driving both business innovation and social change. The chapter examines Walmart's initiatives in harnessing the power of technology to address societal challenges, from enhancing accessibility and affordability to leveraging data for social good. Interviews with tech leaders within the organization shed light on the ongoing efforts to align innovation with positive societal impact.

The reader is invited to consider the evolving expectations of consumers and employees regarding corporate responsibility. The chapter explores how businesses, including Walmart, are adapting their strategies to meet the demands of a socially conscious consumer base and a workforce that values purpose-driven initiatives.

Closing the chapter, the narrative prompts reflection on the symbiosis of leadership, innovation, and social impact. The reader is left with a sense of the interconnected nature of these elements and how they collectively contribute to shaping the trajectory of Walmart and the broader landscape of corporate leadership in the contemporary era.

"Chapter 12: The Intersection of Leadership, Innovation, and Social Impact" serves as a forward-looking exploration, providing a nuanced perspective on the confluence of leadership principles, innovative practices, and the broader societal impact of corporate entities like Walmart. It extends the narrative, offering the reader a contemporary lens through which to view the ongoing evolution of business leadership and its role in shaping a positive societal future.

14

Summary

"Driving Change: Rob Walton's Leadership Journey at Walmart" is a comprehensive exploration of Walmart's evolution under the leadership of Rob Walton. The book unfolds through twelve chapters, covering the early days of Walmart, global expansion, technological challenges, and Walmart's commitment to corporate responsibility. Each chapter offers a detailed examination of the strategic decisions, innovations, and cultural shifts that have defined Walmart's trajectory.

Chapter 1 introduces Rob Walton's leadership journey in the early 1970s, emphasizing his vision for adapting to changing retail dynamics. Subsequent chapters delve into Walmart's global expansion, technological advancements, and corporate responsibility initiatives. The narrative captures the challenges faced by Walmart and Rob Walton's strategic responses, providing a nuanced understanding of the company's growth and evolution.

Chapters 6, 8, and 9 extend the narrative beyond Rob Walton's tenure, exploring Walmart's contemporary strategies, challenges, and innovations. These chapters offer insights into Walmart's response to the ever-evolving retail landscape, incorporating elements such as global market dynamics, technological advancements, and sustainability practices.

The final chapters, 10 through 12, provide a retrospective view of Rob Walton's lasting legacy on Walmart and the retail industry. They examine the enduring impact of his leadership principles, the ongoing evolution of Walmart's strategies, and the intersection of leadership, innovation, and social impact in the 21st century.

The book serves as a comprehensive exploration of Walmart's journey, offering a multi-dimensional view of the company's growth, challenges, and strategic responses. It intertwines Rob Walton's leadership philosophy with the broader narrative of corporate leadership, innovation, and social responsibility, providing the reader with a holistic understanding of Walmart's place in the retail landscape.

www.ingramcontent.com/pod-product-compliance
Lightning Source LLC
LaVergne TN
LVHW010441070526
838199LV00066B/6125